EMAIL MARK[...]

I0021851

List Building and Campaigns

By Paul D. Kings
Copyrights 2017 **Paul D. Kings**

https://www.pauldkings.com

Preface

If you haven't yet started building an email list for your business, this book is for you. A strong email list is one of the most valuable assets you can have. When you're starting from scratch, it's easy to feel overwhelmed or discouraged. Many business owners have a hard time envisioning the long-term payoff for the hard work that is needed now.

If you're serious about growing your business, building a healthy email list should be one of your top priorities. When it comes down to it, your list is one of the only online assets that you have one-hundred percent control over. This book will guide you through all the process you will need to discover how to build a successful and productive email list.

Paul D. Kings

Table of Contents

CHAPTER 1- LIST BUILDING

List Building is the process of creating and maintaining an accurate and up to date list of your contacts email details. The email address is obviously the must have item to add them to your contacts. You want to be as complete as possible, adding their name and other personal details. Any information you have additionally will help you hone your communication with this person and make it feel more personal and engaged.

First you have to have an email address of your own. The registration process is done online with which ever provider you wish, you will find them online with a (.com) suffix like 'providername.com.' You will send the person your email via your email service provider, which is the company you signed up with when you registered, such as Gmail, Hotmail, Yahoo, etc.

Many email service providers are being banned by companies due to their inability to provide a one-hundred percent delivery rate. The largest mail provider is Google (Gmail). Like many others, they provide an free service to sign up. You will just need to enter your contact details as you specify the email address you would like.

This email address is your choice, but with so many personal details already utilized across the globe, you may not get the one you prefer. Most providers will give you an example of a similar and available choice that they can provide. It may be something like 'graham1003' instead of 'graham' to make your email unique to their system.

There is a worldwide standard of the symbol @ (accomplished by pressing shift and 2 at the same time) meaning 'at,' which determines the name of the service provider so in the above example 'graham1003' would be followed by @ meaning 'at' then the service provider name.

Each of the email service providers give the same basic functionality through their screens, but of course each provider will be slightly different. The building of the list of your contacts is provided by your chosen service provider. This would be accomplished by following the prompts to enter all their contact details. Then you will be able to read and send emails from that contact.

You will be requested to provide your identification details like name and address through the series of screens or prompts. With this email account, you will be able to build your email list where you will be able to add other people's contact details using their email details and name and other information you have. You can add to their information and update it as you discover more about your contact.

Another way to get information from your contact is to give that person your details and for them to email you directly. This process will send an email to you and the basic contact details will be available for you to add to your contact list (email list). The next stage will be to add lots more contacts details so you are adding to your list.

Advantages of list building for your business

The World Wide Web made everything a whole lot easier for us to access information. No doubt about that. The continually developing and growing cyber space has bridged all the continents and its multicultural inhabitants together and it is in the palm of your hand. The efficiency of today's telecommunication has enabled each individual to reach those even at the remotest of areas in an instant.

With the confidence that any messages posted online will be seen and heard by this massive audience, the marketing industry has taken a strong interest in this technology. Now, they've come up with a thousand and one ways to earn, advertise, or boost your business' profit.

From selling merchandise, to applying for web related jobs, the internet has became an e-commerce market. There is marketing open for everyone, for every business and every cause. The World Wide Web has utilized its powerful abilities to stretch the popularity of a certain business to a broader and more exact audience.

Email list building is an e-marketing strategy which requires two steps: first is obtaining a client's basic contact information, such as his name an email address, and then establishing a personal digital relationship with these potential buyers.

List building has traditionally come in other forms like telemarketing, fax marketing and mail marketing. Your email contact list is just a modern extension of that same technique.

The main purpose why you would want to build this connection with these contacts is to gain traffic to your site or to point them to your business. You'll send each address important alerts, whether it's in the form of newsletters, online postcards, or an online brochure, about your site or business. It's about feeding them useful information, prompting them to be interested in you and your business and searching for more information about what you provide. If the information you provide turns out to be convincing, then you've got yourself a customer.

Perhaps you are asking yourself, "Isn't that spamming?" No. This strategy is a permission-based notification. Once a potential customer lands on your website and has decided to sign up for your email list or your notifications, they have subscribed to at least one service.

On the other hand, there are potential customers who do not want subscriptions from your site. You just have to make the opt-in box easily seen and make sure it contains a brief and concise description of what they are signing up for.

The key to success is attaining a list of current and correct email addresses. This takes a lot of time, but it can surely turn your business around, whether it is just struggling or close to dying. Your email list is considered powerful if you can engage your potential customers and elicit great responses from them about your site.

Their email addresses should lead you to your target audience as you branch out and from then on, the magic unveils on its own. And since the results come from volume of email addresses, you have the choice to buy another person's or company's list. It is a great idea if you wanted to save time and earn more quickly from your efforts. But, the strength or worth of the list will remain unknown until you've tested it properly.

You need qualified leads, meaning they want what you provide. What if these clients are looking for a different kind of product or are simply disinterested in your product or business? Some "haters" can even report you as a spammer or block your email address.

As mentioned earlier, the key is to build a "trust" filled relationship with prospective clients. Once they've chosen you for your product or business, make sure you'll be able to deliver a hundred and one percent to make them into fans.

Present a colorful, engaging, interactive and informative landing page for your visitors. You want them to easily grasp what you have to offer and how it might benefit them without the direct feeling of being sold something. You have to create a need or want and make them realize that they are missing what you offer.

In email list building, the key is to convince your audience why they need to buy your products or services. Explain what you provide in your emails and that by giving you their information, they granted you permission to send them updates and advertisements to their email address.

How to build an email marketing list

In the world of online business, email contact list building is the process of developing a growing database of contact's email addresses who have an interest in your business and who may be willing to consider buying from you. So how do you build a potential customer list? Here is 5 easy steps to follow.

1. Start With An Email Auto-Responder.

You need reliable auto-responder software when you're building a customer list. An autoresponder can automatically send potential customers a sequence of pre-written templated emails when they subscribe to your list. The software will keep a record of who you send each email campaign to, the subject line, the text within the email, the potential customer's email open rate, the potential customer's rate of clicking on your email (their interaction with your email) and how many messages you have sent to that contact.

2. Put An Opt-In Form On Your Website.

Your email list building strategy starts with an opt-in form. This is a virtual database inclusion form that can easily be created by your autoresponder software. You position the opt-in on your website so that your website visitors can see it and insert their email address. You should only ask for their email address as at this stage, because the more details you ask for with that low level of trust, the less likely people will be to provide you their information.

3. Offer Something of Value For Free.

To encourage the website visitor to provide you with their email address, you will need to offer something of value to them in return. This is how to build your list, in a low trust, coming from a place of giving swap. What you give away for free at this point with their low trust for you, will reflect back on the quality of the products and services that you sell or the services you deliver. So, be creative. Think about the needs of your target customer and fulfill one of their most basic needs with a free report, video or newsletter related to your business. The opt-in freebee should be emailed to the person as soon as they opt-in to your email contact list via your autoresponder.

4. Set Up A Sales Funnel.

Now that the prospective customer is on your email contact list, you need to guide them through the process of understanding the benefits of your products and services. This is your sales funnel or needs-creation funnel. This is a series of messages emailed to your prospect with various product up-sells and down-sells that are meant to create a need in your customer so that you can fulfill that need with your products or services. As you build onto your customer list, a prospective customer will, on average, need to see or hear your marketing messages at least seven times before they take action and buy from you. So, your message has to be interesting, engaging, and effective enough to chip away at their prospective needs for those several times that they hear from you.

5. Always Provide Value.

One of the most important elements of email list building is to constantly deliver value to the people on your contact list. Of course, although your content is directed toward specific reasons to buy your product, their targeted needs, but you don't want to make it sound like a persistent sales pitch. As you deliver valuable information, your potential customers and subscribers will start to trust you and regard you as an expert in your market regarding their potential need. They will then be more likely to buy from you to fulfill that need.

As your email contact database grows, you will need to automate the process. It will become impossible to manage your database manually. It is smart time management to use a reliable email software which can handle many more emails than you could ever process manually. This automation allows you to get back to running your business while it manages your email marketing campaigns.

CHAPTER 2- TARGETED EMAIL MARKETING LIST

Building a targeted email marketing contact list is essential for long-term online business success. If you don't build a list of your potential customers, you are leaving lot of money on the table, because your competitors will be doing this. Those business owners who take the time to build a qualified list can spend only a few minutes creating a single email template in order to reach thousands of people on their targeted list with a needs driven offer. You will swoop in to satisfy a targeted need before your competitor has fulfilled it and sometimes before your customer has even fully realized their need.

Unless you have a very large full-time staff working for you, there is no practical way you can really be effective in your market without building a base of subscribers or potential customers who are willing to receive your targeted email offers which fit their needs.

How to Harvest it For Maximum Profit

Either Way You Look At It, Your Targeted Email Marketing Lists Is A Gold Mine.

Not to exaggerate, but you really can harvest handsome profits with targeted email marketing lists that point customers to your online store or marketplace. All you need to do is market your products or services correctly and ethically. By that, I mean that you must ensure whatever you are offering to your contact list is of the highest quality and value for the targeted potential customer. Also, while you may be a expert in contact list building, the amount of money you can earn depends on the quality of how your list targets the potential customer's needs. After a bit of experience, you will be able to predict your email contact list's response to your campaigns and categorize their potential to buy from you.

1) Targeted Email Marketing Lists Never Die

Yes, targeted email marketing lists methods are still very much alive and productive. In fact, because of increased competition, it is even more important now. If you've heard about these methods, the money is in the quality of the list you create, how targeted it is to your market and your product. Your job as a marketing professional is to maximize your profits by the exact way you communicate with your contact lists. Treat them like your closest business associates or friends and continue to recommend valuable need-targeted products to them. Over time, you will have unconsciously created a sense of trust with them because you are ever-present, never pushy, needs based, and relevant to their lives.

2) There Is Something Wrong If You Are Not Being You

Personal branding is very important if you are building targeted contact email marketing lists for the long term. You can certainly recommend individualized products, but ultimately putting in a pinch of your personality in every email campaign is better. Learn this one skill and skip all the mistakes I've made. People ultimately want to connect. They want their needs met by a person, not a computer.

If you market with your genuine personality, you will attract more customers. Potential customers who like you as a person, will be more favorable to what you have to offer. We have an innate desire to help people we like, so be likable in your emails. Throw in a bit of wit or a quirk or a joke or some humor. Let your contact list know you are a person behind the email and it will pay dividends.

3) Do You Think Its All About the Money?

Finally, while earning money is important, you really want to be able to help others online to fulfill their needs. If you build targeted email marketing contact lists with the intention to only make money, then you probably will end up with just short-term money. This is the sales motto, churn and burn. A marketing person who churns and burns their list will be so busy with the short view of sales and immediate money that they will forget to build strong long term relationships to gain referrals and business supporters.

You must position your products or services toward being able to serve others, to come from contribution in all your actions. In one way or another, your product or service needs to be geared toward helping people to get what they want in life and making the potential customer into a 'true fan' of your business. They will tolerate your emails through the period of time that they don't need your products or services and keep receiving the emails until the need is there for them to do business with you.

The true marketing professional will assess the needs of his or her potential customer and meet that need, whether the need will be present today or next week. They are the ones who will earn the referrals of friends today, the sales tomorrow, and will reap the benefits long term over the relationship.

Another targeting technique is to watch the interaction with your contact email lists, categorizing your potential customers based on their behavior, with click rates and other metrics, as an A customer, meaning ready to buy now, B customer, ready to buy soon but not now, and C customer, a late adopter, who will wait for a sale or for a holiday to prompt them to buy.

Buying An Email Marketing List, Worth It or Worth-less?

Now you've learned how invaluable an email campaign is to promote your product, service, business or affiliate sales products. Your next task is to build a contact list to which you will begin to send emails. The question is, where do you get the list from? Many people think that things would be easier if they just buy a email contact marketing list. Don't be one of the people who make that expensive mistake.

You may have seen the ads that offer to provide you with thousands of email address for a very low cost. There's a reason they are providing so much for so little. If you fall for the hype and purchase one of these email marketing lists, you'll most likely be labeled as a 'spammer' right after you send out your first batch of emails and your email address will be worthless to those contacts and will be contaminated within the server because Gmail and other email providers will have blocked your email address as Spam.

Most of the messages will most likely end up in the junk email category and you won't reap the desired benefits from your efforts. More than likely, about 70% of the addresses are bogus or duplicated or sold so many times that the targeting potential is lost. While the other 30% of the email contact addresses haven't given anyone permission to email messages to them, so they will become angry at getting your message without their permission.

Some people use a paid email contact list from various submission services, because they are trying to speed up their marketing. These email contact lists can end up costing between 20 and 30 cents per individual email, which are not likely to be your target customers for your product.

So what can you do instead? Perhaps reading the next several ideas will get the ideas flowing about how you can build your own targeted customer email list. Keep in mind that your primary goal should be to send emails to potential customers who really want to hear what you have to say and are open to doing business with you, now or in the future.

The big question is 'where do you find these targeted potential customers?' Your best bet at the beginning is to use a diverse group of marketing methods (the shotgun approach, start broad and narrow from there) and then watch your web traffic and the responses you get.

Below you will find a list of procedures, shared by an existing email marketing company, of the steps which will help ensure you have success building your email contact marketing list.

1. Use Your Webpage - On every page of your website should request that individuals sign up, a basic call-to-action. You can offer in exchange for their email, your online electronic magazine, your newsletter, your free report on a targeted subject, a small e-book, or some other item that has a perceived value to the reader.

2. Consider Direct Mail Marketing – You can use snail mail (postal mail) to send card stock postcards or flyers to all of your potential customers. In the design of your mailer campaign, include a request for people to visit your website and sign up for the valued information you're offering.

3. Think about using Telemarketers - You could use a telemarketing service or agent to contact your potential clients. Your telemarketers should require email addresses when they make a qualified contact or believe someone is your target customer. You can offer incentives, like coupons or free trials, entry into a contest, or something else that they'd want, to those who supply their email address.

Beware, people are likely to give you an email address that they have created just for spam if they feel pressured or hassled in any way, so make sure the telemarketer is very polite and respectful. Otherwise you will just get junk information from the process. As they say in customer qualification, garbage in, garbage out. So you want to have people actually engaged in the process and to WANT contact from you, so they give you their most used email address.

4. Use a Broker - Brokerage services are websites that offer heavy internet traffic. They cull information from hundreds to thousands of target specific sites and can sell that information to you about your potential customers. Because it culls the customers looking for the targeted business, it is a better idea to get customer information from them. Basically, it is 'use our search engine" and then input your information and their online service pairs the customer with their target business type. It is free to the customer, but to the business wanting their customer email list, this usually costs between $.10 and $.15 for each email address.

For example, if I put in 'property management services' into Google, dozens of search websites and websites that offer pairing you with property management services will be the result. On the back end, property management services pay them to connect the customer searching for property management with their company, either per email address or per qualified lead.

5. Use Good Ole' Pavement Action - You can have students who are off in the summer or on one of their school breaks go door-to-door offering information in exchange for their email addresses. The point is to create trust. Who doesn't want to help out a student who is there on their doorstep? So, you are garnering the inherent trust of person-to-person action in order to leverage your email contact list kick start.

6. Host an Online Contest - Open contests held on your website or social media page are a very effective way to get people to share their email addresses with you. In the case of social media, it gets you a wealthy of information on the individuals who leave their privacy settings open to the public.

On the entry form on your website, require that they their email address to you as their way of entering the contest toward the prize. Even if they don't win, make sure to sent the congratulatory email for the winner out to all on your email contact list, this garners trust that the contest was for real and it also gets your product, service, and name in front of them one more time.

7. Get Physical - If you have an actual brick and mortar store, ask your customers to provide you with their email address during your checkout process. Inform them that they will receive emails with coupons, discounts, special events, or surveys. You could also run additional more targeted contests to keep them engaged.

8 - You Choose What Fits Your Style- The suggestions you have been given should've opened up some new avenues in your mind or at least reinforced what you should do, but right now haven't been getting done. It is time for you to fill in the method that would work best for you at this time, at this place in your business development, and with your budget of time and money.

As you can see there are several routes to arrive at the same destination - acquiring good, targeted email addresses for your email marketing campaign.

But, to answer the question of whether to buy an email marketing list - NO! Absolutely not.

Paul D. Kings

CHAPTER 3- LIST BUILDING AND SOCIAL MEDIA

The real value of list building with social media is in your ability to create a brand and an image to a targeted set of potential customers with incredible reach. The opportunity for you to build a highly responsive list using different social media platforms is enormous. However, but for all its potential, there is one simple, but far too often overlooked, critical secret to list building with social media--authenticity.

Being authentic is the essence of Attraction Marketing and it is the single most important success factor for your marketing efforts. The problem with lots of social media campaigns is that it is a new platform but the old high pressure, low trust building techniques. The potential for Attraction Marketing is that you can target your most likely potential customers in a friendly, person and need-centric environment, have a low pressure, and high gentle contact environment.

Why be different? Because so few people marketing their business using social media are actually authentic - just look at your Twitter page if you need proof. What percentage of the posts you see in your active Twitter stream offer any value to you as a follower? What percentage of posts do you see in your active Twitter stream outright offer some product link you care nothing about? They are using a new technology to do sales the old way.

The truth is that the bar has been set very, very low in the social media environment. It is easy for you to stand out as an attraction marketer when you choose to be authentic and personal. Being authentic enables you to build a relationship on a solid foundation in which people can begin to know you, like you and trust you. Because the gain with social media is that everything is shared from friend to friend and group to group, you multiply your reach by being friendly, authentic, and helpful.

The bottom line with social media is simple. It's one of the only arenas where you can actually generate a great income by being your best self. And when you are being yourself, you are being authentic. The Merriam-Webster dictionary defines being authentic as "being true to one's own personality, spirit, or character."

When building your online presence, it is imperative that you are being yourself---or the best version of yourself that you can be, maybe a little more upbeat, a bit more informative, a little more friendly. You will represent your brand wholeheartedly while being honest with your audience, and your followers will seek you out and share you with their friends. Express your passions and beliefs and allow your personality to shine through--and people will want to hear what you have to say.

For great examples of how this has worked, take a look at Seth Godin and Tim Ferriss. They leveraged their personality into a brand and they have people begging for more and signing up for their next thing before it is even produced. They made their personality the basis for their brand. If someone likes them, then the potential customer is willing to trust them on multiple subjects or products, such as diet supplements, books, exercise, cook books, etc.

Effective Method to Build Your Email and Contact List with social media

These days, social media plays a very important role in contact and customer list building and in direct internet marketing. Social media sites like Twitter and Facebook have billions of subscribers. This means that the number of people you can potentially add to your targeted customer list also has no practical limit.

Since communication and connection, either with family or friends, has become very important to most people, you can use this as your leverage to draw them to your site. You can add their friends and family from their profile page. When they see you have mutual connections, they won't think twice about adding you to their social media circle.

If you are able to do this, slowly and carefully, without angering the social media bots for adding people too quickly or getting marked as spam, then there really is no limit to the number of people you can reach with your site or can connect to. The more targeted people you connect to in a meaningful way, the more opportunities for profit.

Another thing you need to consider is the number of times you connect with your targeted customer list. Frequency is very important because it helps build name recognition and trust. If you will be advertising your products and services one time and then stopping, don't expect a high profit or robust outcome.

As a matter of fact, don't expect a profit at all. One and done is not an effective way to earn money online, remember that is the short term look at marketing which sacrifices today's profit at the expense of future relationships. Successful Internet marketers connect with their list as often as they can in order to achieve their target, which is mutual need satisfaction.

Then again, what is targeted list building? How can it help you succeed in your Internet marketing campaigns? Building a list refers to the process of subscribing a targeted audience to engage and draw in to the brand, product, or service you represent. With this process, you need to be creative and you need to learn to customize to your target audience in order to succeed.

There are great ways to ensure a successful email and social media list building. These ways can be of great advantage to both bloggers and regular website owners. Here are some of them:

Ning social networks - This is a great way to connect with other members of the Ning network. You can broadcast messages and interact with other people. Successful internet marketers mention that subscribing to Ning can be powerful because it offers email broadcast capability, social network integration, and member sign in via Facebook and other social networks. So, without a lot of know-how, you can have a fully integrated site which can capture social media login profiles in a passive, high context environment.

Autoresponder - We all know that before we can subscribe to a popular website or to any website for that matter, we need to sign up with our email address. So who ever mentioned that having an email account is antiquated has not seen the potential of targeted email marketing. Email marketing is still the best way to target qualified subscribers, they want you as much as you want them. With an autoresponder, you can connect with your subscribers on a more personal tone and more often than you would generally think to do so. You set up a campaign, put the target into that campaign and let it do its magic.

Facebook Fan Page or Twitter – One billion subscribers use Facebook daily. That's one-seventh of the planet's people. The popularity and frequent login is to your advantage.

Who still doesn't know about Facebook? Better yet - Who still doesn't have a Facebook account? Let's face it, computer or no computer; Internet connection or none; 18 years old or not, almost everyone has an FB account. Even small kids fake their ages just to subscribe because of FB games like FarmVille, Ninja Saga and Social City.

Your posts alone can draw in comments from members, so keep your posts light, humorous, interesting, engaging, and sharable. This is a great way to brand yourself and to get your product message out there. The same goes for a Twitter account (except for the games but many people find it a great way to follow their favorite celebrities).

Google Friend Connect - Google has finally made an attempt to add a social element to every site they have. With Google newsletters, you can email the other subscribers in your group, taking advantage of their opt-in and trust that has already been established.

There are other ways to succeed in email and social media list building. Aside from the ones mentioned above, you can also make use of RSS subscriptions. (Rich Site Summary, often called Really Simple Syndication) uses a simple web feed format to send out frequently updated content such as blog articles, syndicated news headlines, customized audio files, and targeted videos. With social media becoming more sophisticated in the way you can connect with people, building a list of ⬚uality subscribers has never been easier.

Article Marketing and List Building

Article marketing and list building allows you to have a small list and enjoy big profit from hyper responsive well targeted customers. So I've got really good news for you here that I think you're going to enjoy, and you will want to take action on immediately.

Here's the good news:

You don't need a large list for success online---you need a quality, targeted, needs-based list.

"What? But everybody tells me the money's in the size of the list. I've got to have a huge list."

That's only half correct. Yes, the money is in the list. The half that is not correct is that you need a large list. You do need a targeted list, a correct list, a needs based list, and motivated buyer list.

Now, when I go to speak at Internet marketing seminars, or attend internet marketing seminars, people are always walking around talking about the size of their list, like I should be impressed. I would never win any of those comparisons because my list is not about being huge in the numbers of potential targets. I don't have millions of people on my list. What I do have are highly responsive people who are engaged with me and want my products who are on my list.

We'll get to that in just a minute. So calm down, relax. You don't have to build a huge list. That's the good news. So don't let anybody fool you that you have to get it bigger and bigger and bigger and bigger. Anyone can build a huge list. You can buy a list of lots of lines of people's email information, for that matter, but they may not -- and are usually not hyper responsive people who want your stuff.

What You Want is a Hyper Responsive List

Now, let's talk about that word 'list' for a minute. We use strange words on the Internet. A list sounds like just this impersonal group of names or e-mail addresses that you don't care about. That's why I call my list, my list community, which reminds me to treat them like I would a physical community.

My list community is a community of people who have chosen to learn from me. It's my responsibility to take care of them and treat them like my community, my friends, my trusted customers. This is part of what creates a hyper responsive list. When you take care of your community, when you give them good stuff, in exchange then you get a hyper responsive customer list.

What that **doesn't** involve is bombing them every day with the latest and greatest new offer. It makes sure you are not spamming them with that thing that's going to make them $1M before they go to bed that night and other such scams. No, that's not how you create a hyper responsive list. That's how you create a list of people bothered by you and ignoring your attempts to contact.

The Good News Continued

All you need is a small, highly qualified hyper responsive list of super fans. One of the reasons that I frequently win, or at least place in the top five of the affiliate contests is because my list is hyper responsive. They trust me, because I've taken good care of them and feel that I am out there gathering information for them and delivering it to them without effort.

So you want to take really good care of your contact list by giving them good information, answering their questions, and asking them questions about what they struggle with and need. That's how you create a hyper responsive list. You find out what they need and then you supply it.

With a Highly Qualified List

One of the ways to create a highly qualified list is with article marketing, with getting small samples of your content out there to potential prospects. So in your article you demonstrate how you approach solving problems and some potential problem solutions. In that three to five minutes which it takes them to read an article, as opposed to four lines on a Google ad, they've read useful information, they've begun to be engaged and to know, like, and trust you.

When you do it properly, by the end of the article they're thinking that they would like some more information from you. And boom, there's a handy call to action in your resource box, which is inviting them to get more information from you.

So that's how you get a highly qalified contact list. You nurture your contacts and take great care of your list to turn it into a hyper responsive list community. In summary, small list, big profits, with a hyper responsive list community.

About the Author, Paul D. Kings

Paul D. Kings is a software engineer by trade, and a father, husband, and self-published author. He likes to write about selling and making money online. Paul has been selling on eBay and Amazon since 2007.

Visit Paul's website at https://www.pauldkings.com

Want to Read More?
Find my other books at:
https://www.pauldkings.com

Free Training:

"How to Earn a 6-Figure Side-Income Online"

One Last Thing...

If you enjoyed this book or found it useful, I'd be very grateful if you'd post a short review on Amazon. Your support really does make a difference and I read all my reviews personally so I can get your feedback and make this book even better.

Thanks again for your support!

www.ingramcontent.com/pod-product-compliance
Lightning Source LLC
Chambersburg PA
CBHW070903070326
40690CB00009B/1975